INSTANT
Style

D0959722

Cho, Emily.
Instant style : 500
professional tips on
c1996.
33305009303078
CA   01/27/99

INSTANT

Style

500 PROFESSIONAL

TIPS ON FASHION,

BEAUTY, AND ATTITUDE

EMILY CHO
&
NEILA FISHER

Illustrations by Cheryl Lickona

SANTA CLARA COUNTY LIBRARY

3 3305 00930 3078

INSTANT STYLE. Copyright © 1996 by Emily Cho and Neila Fisher. All rights reserved. Printed in the United States of America. No part of this book may be used or reproduced in any manner whatsoever without written permission except in the case of brief quotations embodied in critical articles and reviews. For information address HarperCollins Publishers, Inc., 10 East 53rd Street, New York, NY 10022.

HarperCollins books may be purchased for educational, business, or sales promotional use. For information please write: Special Markets Department, HarperCollins Publishers, Inc., 10 East 53rd Street, New York, NY 10022.

FIRST EDITION

Designed by Gloria Adelson/LuLu Graphics
Design Assistant: Ruth Lee
Illustrations by Cheryl Lickona

Library of Congress Cataloging-in-Publication Data

Cho, Emily.
    Instant style : 500 professional tips on fashion, beauty, and
  attitude / Emily Cho and Neila Fisher ; illustrations by
  Cheryl Lickona. — 1st ed.
        p.   cm.
    ISBN 0–06–273399–0
    1. Clothing and dress.   2. Beauty, Personal.   I. Fisher, Neila.
  II. Title.
  TT507.C54   1996
  646'.34—dc20   95-46584

---

96 97 98 99 00 ❖/RRD 10 9 8 7 6 5 4 3 2 1

To our readers,

All the advice in this book has come from our years of working with clients, answering every question under the sun on fashion, beauty, and style.

We're asked about these things so often that we decided to write this book and share the answers with you.

Have a great time with the tips. We had a great time collecting them.

INSTANT
Style

1: Several days before a trip, take out a pad of paper and make a list of all the items you'll need. Each time you remember something you want to bring, add it to the list. Check off each item when you pack.

2: Stiff sprayed hair is dated. Run your fingers through your hair after spraying it to soften the style. You'll have the same look, but it will be current.

3: Use your favorite color to get yourself out of a bad mood or to evoke a mood in others.

4: Sexy dressing is totally individual. Focus on your strengths—elegant legs, tiny waist, curved hips, rounded rear, cleavage, or a combination of them all if you're that lucky.

5: Be leery of wearing sunglasses when there is no sunlight. They look at best theatrical, at worst intimidating.

6: Never split up a suit—the separate pieces won't look as good with any other partners as they look together.

7: From working with our clients, we've found that there are two clothing personalities. One type is happier with fewer and better clothes while the other prefers quantity and variety. Both personalities are fine.

8: For a lift, add a belt to an outfit; it defines and contours, and it can add a touch of color or texture.

9: The perfect jacket covers the rear and gives a longer line to the body.

10: Try not to get hung up on one outfit or look just because it's easy. Change and variety are worth the effort.

11: If you look good, the product you're selling looks better. That product could be a computer, a book, or yourself! We're all selling something.

12: Use concealer to camouflage facial lines around the nose and mouth. Dot concealer over foundation directly in the groove of the line and gently blend.

13: You should keep the following items in your emergency travel kit and in your desk.

- **clear nail polish (for stocking runs)**

- **nail file**

- **cuticle scissors**

- **extra pairs of neutral and black hose**

- **safety pins for hiding unwanted straps and falling hems**

- **small sewing kit**

- **shoulder pads**

- **all-purpose pair of earrings**

14: If you have family jewelry to wear, take advantage of it: It will help you create an original look.

15: The weather is hot and you're wearing dark colors because you're feeling over-weight—make sure the fabric is lightweight.

16: If you're big busted, go for the best mini-mizer bra; they really work.

17: For a plane trip, carry a separate little plas-tic bag filled with conveniences such as socks, toothpaste and a toothbrush, a contact lens case, light perfume, moisturizer, a spray bottle of spring water, and refreshing eye drops.

18: If you have narrow shoulders, wear halter necklines to give an illusion of greater width.

19: Camouflage a wide waist with clothing that has no defined waistline, like a shift or a tunic.

20: Quality is:

no puckering at the seams

soft yet durable pockets and lining fabric

stitches that don't show through to the outside

an even hemline

21: *Over the long haul, if you're blessed with good skin, you've got the most valuable asset, so take care of it. Even we can't buy beautiful skin for you.*

22: A mid-calf skirt creates an instant arty look.

23: A "non-earring"—a sporty earring, such as a small coin or stud—comes in very handy when you want to look casual yet finished.

24: An accessory can hold a garment together physically while adding pizzazz. A long heavy chain draped on a plunging neckline of a blouse will add weight to hold the material in place.

25: If your upper arm is heavy, you can still wear a short sleeve if the sleeve is long enough to hide the heaviest part.

wwwwwwwwwwwwwwwwwwwwwwwwwwwwwwwwwwwwww

26: *We think giving unsolicited fashion or beauty advice is inappropriate.*

wwwwwwwwwwwwwwwwwwwwwwwwwwwwwwwwwwwwww

27: The most aging behavior is a tired walk. Remember to move gracefully.

28: If you're short, wear simple lines—you don't have enough display area for anything complicated.

29: In a corporate setting, don't wear cutesy floral or animal-print motifs.

30: Eyebrows form a natural outline for your face and accent and emphasize your eyes. It's usually best to follow the natural line when you tweeze them. If they need extra definition, use brown or taupe eye shadow applied with a thin brush. Try to create a soft arch.

31: Hats can be intimidating; however, the right hat can be your signature.

32: *You don't like your body? We've hardly had a client who did. If you've tried the gyms and the diet fads and you just can't lose the weight, then learn to live with it. There are many camouflages to take advantage of, like shoulder pads to balance wide hips.*

33: Pick out new sunglasses to feel instantly chic and today.

34: If you're petite, large prints or too much fabric will make you look even smaller.

35: Wearing color is the quickest way to get a compliment from a man.

36: Sets: Whenever a bottom has a matching top or a sweater has a matching oversweater, buy both pieces. Sets expand your wardrobe more than you can imagine. You'll look instantly pulled together.

37: When in doubt about choosing a pump, the Chanel look (black toe, beige pump) will probably work fine.

38: If you want to wear a print, wear it with solids. Coordinating two patterns calls for a sophisticated eye. You can, of course, rely on the designers' eyes when they coordinate several patterns in one outfit.

39: Don't ever put your hem length at the thickest part of your leg—be it calf, ankle, or above the knee. Adjust the hem so that it falls to a more slender part of your leg.

40: Mix some femininity with your practicality: Get a swinging georgette skirt to wear with your suit jacket.

41: Leave more than enough time in your schedule to get to an appointment. You'll avoid looking frazzled.

42: Have that one staple dinner dress so you never have to shop frantically to meet a last-minute invitation. You'll know you have a uniform in which you can feel great.

43: Put all your bundles into one large, neat black tote bag so you don't look like a bag lady.

44: A make-it-through-the-work-week wardrobe includes:

> **two jackets: one solid, one tweed or checked**
>
> **three skirts: two solid, one patterned**
>
> **four blouses: two white or cream, two colored**
>
> **two coats: one raincoat—tan, one wool top-coat—probably black, brown, or navy**

45: To save their shape, remove shoulder pads before cleaning a shirt, jacket, or dress. You'll be able to reattach them quickly with two tiny safety pins.

46: When buying a bright, outstanding color or print, keep the line of the outfit simple to balance the drama of the color.

47: Sexy dressing might mean low-cut, but unless you are comfortable in it, it is no good.

48: For the care of your skin, have on hand: moisturizer, eye cream, night cream, eye makeup remover, tweezers, and a magnifying mirror.

49: Buy the best handbag you can afford; it will help your image. It's a focal point and lifts the level of your entire outfit with its message of quality.

50: Underwear should match your skin tone, not your clothing color.

~~~~~~

51: Balance is a sophisticated lesson in the art of dressing. For example, if you come across as intimidating, dress down and use your clothes to put people more at ease.

~~~~~~

52: A great habit is to get dressed and put on makeup first thing every morning—you'll feel ready for anything.

53: A print can reveal a lot about you. A person in a geometric print appears to be more orderly and predictable. The person in a wild colorful print sends a message of flair and excitement.

54: Long blouses are sometimes difficult to tuck into pants and skirts because of their bulk. Shorten them. Just make sure you can lift your arms high without the blouse coming out of the waistband.

55: Understated is still best. Have one special suit in a dressier fabric, like a wool crepe, and only wear it to events like an office party. It's a dressier version of the look that you usually project and will be easily accepted.

56: For heavy ankles, dark-tinted hose in taupe or black are a must.

57: Soft textures like angora and cashmere can feminize an outfit.

〰〰〰〰〰〰〰〰〰〰〰〰〰〰〰〰〰〰〰〰〰〰〰〰〰〰

58: *We think of your hair color and hair-style as a most important accessory. You can change it often, or it can be your signature.*

〰〰〰〰〰〰〰〰〰〰〰〰〰〰〰〰〰〰〰〰〰〰〰〰〰〰

59: For instant unique, toss a geometric scarf over a checked jacket.

60: The quickest way to be fashionable is to wear a single-color top and bottom. We prefer the palette of core colors: black, beige, cream, brown, or navy. You can then layer it with any color jacket or shawl.

61: Style Fact: Thin fabrics like silk crepe or wool jersey fall better and are more slimming than bulky fabrics like wool tweed and suede.

62: For the best eyelash look, apply mascara from base to tip, stroking evenly. Comb through with an eyelash comb. Reapply for a thicker look.

63: Have two sun hats: a great straw one for your pretty dresses and a fold-up cotton one to keep in your bag so you'll always be protected.

64: The look of three solid colors can be very striking. If you're wearing two bright colors together, black is a safe third color.

65: We tell our clients: When you want to really study yourself in the mirror, it's helpful not to look into your eyes. Stay objective. Study the image in the mirror as if it were someone else.

66: If you have a tummy, always blouson your top by pulling a little extra out of your waistband to disguise it and then wear a third layer of a long open jacket or a vest.

67: Wearing different combinations of colors evokes totally different responses. If you like the interesting effect of two colors together and only one is flattering, that is the one to wear next to your face.

68: If you really need your hair to stay in place, use gel and then some hair spray to set it.

69: If your best asset is your legs:

> **Always wear a tapered, short skirt hemmed to the most flattering point on your leg's curve**
>
> **Wear tights with a long sweater that covers your hips**
>
> **Wear high heels—but never so high that you can't walk gracefully**
>
> **Wear sheer hose in the right shade of beige, taupe, or black**

70: For day into evening, change to very sheer hose. Before you do, remember to use some body lotion on your hands and feet for a luxurious feeling and as a money saver—it prevents runs.

~~~~~~

71: *We tell clients, before a new haircut:*

> ***Stand up so your hairdresser can see your proportions***
>
> ***Bring photos of hairstyles you like—don't expect your hairdresser to read your mind***
>
> ***Ask if the styles are possible for your type of hair***
>
> ***Ask if the styles work with your ability for upkeep***

~~~~~~

72: Always tone your stockings to your shoes, not to your skirts. Your legs will look longer.

73: If you have a tummy, never wear a skirt that isn't softened by a sarong tie or soft front pleats. A wrap skirt is also good.

74: Before you buy a fragile item, make sure you're willing to put up with the necessary upkeep, be it frequent ironing or large cleaning bills.

75: We set our own facial lines. Remember that when you squint, wrinkle your forehead, frown, or purse your lips. Relax your facial expressions.

76: The inside organization of your purse should tell the world who you are. Accessories are a mini picture of your taste level. Fashion begins from the inside out.

77: If your skin is extra dry, apply bath oil to your slightly damp body. It lasts and lasts. But be sure the fragrance works with your perfume.

~~~~~~

78: *Complimenting others when they look wonderful makes you appear self-confident.*

~~~~~~

79: Whenever you buy a necklace, buy earrings that will finish the look. Be sure that the mood of the pieces and their metal finish match.

80: If you are large, avoid expansive, bold patterns as well as tiny floral prints.

81: Makeup Note: A line inside the eye rim makes the eye look smaller, whereas a line right under the lower lashes makes the eye look bigger.

82: If you are short, keep color in one family tone, including stockings and shoes. Contrasts break up height.

83: Be sure to match your colors in daylight. Different fabrics pick up the same dye shade differently (e.g., there are many, many shades of black).

〰〰〰〰〰〰〰〰〰〰〰〰〰〰〰〰〰〰〰〰〰〰〰〰〰

84: *Develop your own list of experts: a hairdresser, a special salesperson, a tailor. The bigger your list, the easier putting it all together will be.*

〰〰〰〰〰〰〰〰〰〰〰〰〰〰〰〰〰〰〰〰〰〰〰〰〰

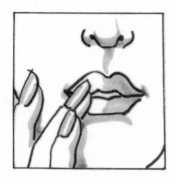

85: To keep your lipstick from bleeding and to keep it on longer:

> **Powder your lips lightly**
>
> **Line your lips with a sharp lip liner**
>
> **After applying your lipstick, blot gently**

86: Don't forget hand lotion on elbows and knees. They need it the most.

~~~~~~

87: After cleaning out a lot of closets, we've come to the conclusion that the only clothes that should be in your closet are those that make you feel good.

~~~~~~

88: To add volume, using a round brush and a heated blow dryer, roll hair under and then back away from your face in two steps.

89: If you're large, avoid too stiff fabrics as well as too flimsy fabrics.

90: If inserting or removing contact lenses, be extra gentle when pulling the skin under your eyes. Constant pulling can cause drooping skin and a baggy look.

91: Air your clothes and make all necessary alterations before putting them back in the closet. Every item in your closet should be in tip-top shape, ready to pull out and wear. You don't want to give yourself any last-minute surprises.

92: Towel-dry your hair until it is just damp before using a blow dryer—you're wasting time if your hair is soaking wet.

93: The moment you get a stain on your clothing, dab it with a little club soda to loosen it up and make it easier for the dry cleaner to get out. Sometimes it will come out completely. Never use water in place of club soda because it sets many stains.

94: Lacy lingerie can slip you into a feminine mood.

95: Only your top or your bottom can be loose and baggy, never both together, except for a sweat suit.

96: If your lips are your best feature, then show them off with exciting choices of color. Try the extremes of bold red for evening and the palest of pales for day. Make them shine with a touch of highlight in gold or a pearlized shade in the middle of your lower lip.

97: A perfume that is more exotic than your daytime scent will put you in an evening mood.

98: When you are feeling dowdy, add a touch of an odd, interesting color to your outfit. Always make it look very deliberate by wearing a second touch of that same color or a shade close to it.

99: Comfort is putting a snap on a too-low-cut blouse.

100: If you apply a thin, thin layer of Vaseline before you use a facial depilatory, there is less chance of redness or irritation.

101. *In our fashion experience, universal instant style has always been—and we think will always be—the little black dress. Be creative and make it your own. Some of the variations we like are:*

a huge, gold belt buckle

layers and layers of pearls

one enormous cuff bracelet

an oversized pin on the shoulder

a multistrand choker

and always *only one of the above at a time*

102: If you want the focus to be on your waist:

Wear a dress, jacket, or top that wraps around your waist

Wear any belt, especially a wide contrasting one

Wear a high-waisted skirt or pants

〰〰〰〰〰〰〰〰〰〰〰〰〰〰〰〰〰〰〰〰〰〰〰〰〰〰〰〰〰

103: *The right clothes give the most valuable message: You are comfortable with yourself!*

〰〰〰〰〰〰〰〰〰〰〰〰〰〰〰〰〰〰〰〰〰〰〰〰〰〰〰〰〰

104: Don't dye shoes to match; it's dated. A dulled silver, gold, or bronze will always be better.

105: There is nothing more irritating than a jagged fingernail that ruins a stocking. Always, always carry an emery board.

〰〰〰〰〰〰〰〰〰〰〰〰〰〰〰〰〰〰〰〰〰〰〰〰〰〰〰〰〰

106: *Do as we do. If you spot someone with a super haircut, outfit, or makeup, stop her and ask about it. Chances are she'll be flattered and you'll learn something.*

〰〰〰〰〰〰〰〰〰〰〰〰〰〰〰〰〰〰〰〰〰〰〰〰〰〰〰〰〰

107: Wear flat shoes if you feel your skirt or pants are on the short side.

108: For everyday use, choose a closed handbag instead of an open tote. They're less accessible and less tempting.

109: Items you shouldn't borrow include: hairbrushes, lipsticks, lip liners, and all real jewelry.

110: When you want a change from suits, there is nothing like a dress for instant femininity. Whenever dresses are in fashion, grab the opportunity to get one because their popularity with designers comes and goes.

~~~~~~

__111:__ If you're spending more than ten minutes choosing and putting together your outfit in the morning, there's something wrong with your wardrobe or your closet organization. We believe your closet should be as organized as you would want your desk to be.

~~~~~~

112: Hairstyle choices include classic, short and sleek, or glamorous. Deliberately make your hair fit one of them.

113: If you are long-waisted, don't blouson your tops.

114: Quick Balance Trick: The more petite you are, the fewer accessories you should wear.

115: To feel more dramatic, wear drop earrings, but not to the office.

116: The best way to hide dark circles under your eyes is to apply foundation first and then layer a lighter-color concealer under your eye with a soft sponge. Place the concealer more toward the nose. This will draw focus away from the actual dark circles.

117: When someone says classic colors to you, they mean brown, beige, navy, gray, black, cream, and white. If you put your wardrobe together in these colors, your clothing will take you further.

118: We think one of the best fashion attributes "you are born with" is a great pair of shoulders.

119: Never wear black lace pantyhose any-where around work. We don't even like them for play. They give too much of an underwear feeling and they don't flatter the leg. (And your feet hurt inside your shoes.)

120: If possible, alter your too-boxy jackets to contour to your body. They'll be much more flattering.

121: When you have no time to change, a fresh flower on your jacket works beautifully for a last-minute date, dinner, or any special event.

122: Before each season, take your shoes to the shoemaker and ask to have them made to look new. The shoemaker can absolutely revive old shoes, even repainting worn black suede.

123: If you can hear your own accessory, like a jangling bracelet or earrings, don't wear it—others can hear it, too.

124: Great Balance Trick: If you are dark haired, wear black shoes; if you are light haired, wear taupe.

125: If narrow shoulders bother you, wear shoulder pads (as wide out on your shoulders as possible) even though they may not be in fashion.

ᗯᗯᗯᗯᗯᗯᗯᗯᗯᗯᗯᗯᗯᗯᗯᗯᗯᗯᗯᗯᗯᗯᗯᗯᗯᗯᗯᗯ

126: *When asked which is more important, we believe comfort comes before fashion. Take the time to try on a dress, for instance, so you'll never have to hold a too-low neckline closed. If you're clutching at your clothes, no one will notice how good you look.*

ᗯᗯᗯᗯᗯᗯᗯᗯᗯᗯᗯᗯᗯᗯᗯᗯᗯᗯᗯᗯᗯᗯᗯᗯᗯᗯᗯᗯ

127: In summer, keep your perfume in the refrigerator. As you are rushing out the door, dab on a refreshing scent.

128: Don't despair if you have brown spots on your hands. The heavy-duty medical concealers really cover them and don't rub off on clothing.

129: If you collect small scarves in colors and prints, you'll have bright accents to tuck in a pocket.

130: For a look of authority, closed pumps are more appropriate than open-toed slingbacks with tailored suits.

131: Focus Rule: Don't put all the emphasis on your good feature if it exposes a bad one. For instance, a wide belt to show off a small waist is not smart if it also makes your hips look much wider.

132: If you're short-waisted, keep to one color rather than contrasts. If you have the choice, your belt should match your top, not your bottom.

133: Cheap Advice: Drink as much water as you can. There is nothing better for your skin!

134: From May to September, get out of your black leather shoes and try patent leather or a lighter color.

135: A money-saving hint is to look for evening-wear possibilities in the lingerie department, such as a satin camisole or a lacy bodysuit.

136: Sometimes one change—be it a new haircut, new hair color, new makeup palette, or, certainly, a big weight change—will affect the way you feel in some of your existing wardrobe. Be prepared to add and drop a few looks.

137: A big white shirt tied at the waist or hip can be a great bathing-suit coverup. It looks casual and current.

138: A large, beautiful print scarf can become a hip wrap or a shawl, as well as a filler for a neckline or a brightener under the collar of a coat.

139: One of Our Image Rules: Catch yourself reflected in a store window and you'll really see who you are.

140: If you are long-waisted, your belt should not be the same color as your top. A contrasting belt is better.

141: Collect jackets in jewel tones like magenta or teal. These jackets can take on an instant evening look when worn over black pants or a black skirt.

142: The trick to using hair spray to add body and volume is to spray your hair at the roots.

143: In cold weather, a thin silk undershirt under your blouse can sometimes keep you warm enough to wear a jacket instead of a coat.

144: For an instant hair lift: Bend over, brush your hair forward, and then flip your head back and softly smooth your hair with your brush.

145: Add a belt anytime your clothes are "running away" from your body. A belt can always secure a garment to your shape.

146: Don't buy a perfume on impulse. Have the store spray the scent on a piece of paper or onto your skin and see how long you love it before you invest.

~~~~~~

147: We observe fashion and style connections in our image work. Typically, the person projecting the better taste will usually be projecting the most power.

~~~~~~

148: Keep at least five favorite scarves—different sizes, colors, and patterns—to help you change the mood of your outfits.

149: The following is a list of essential makeup tools:

foundation

concealer

blending sponge

eyelash curler

mascara

eyeliner pencil

eye pencil sharpener

eyebrow brush

eye shadows

eye makeup brush

blush

blusher brush

lipliner

lipsticks

translucent powder

150: There are eyedrops for red, tired eyes. Check with your pharmacist.

151: If you want the statement of real jewelry, you can get away with buying one great gold necklace and a pair of gold earrings. You can wear them as signature pieces with everything.

152: When you want to be noticed, wear a great color. It is the easiest way to be seen and remembered.

153: That novelty button on a blouse or dress must be considered when you accessorize. If it makes things difficult, don't buy the item.

154: Throw a muffler around your neck, put on matching gloves, and you'll be warm enough in a suit to leave your coat at home.

155: Never wear a two-piece bathing suit if you have even the slightest spare tire.

156: *Sometimes our clients are too con-
servative. Wear that strong color or that
bold accessory and make your statement.
Don't be afraid to stand out—be afraid
not to.*

mmmmmmmmmmmmmmmmmmmmmmmmmmmmmm

157: While your hair is still wet, use hair gel.
Then place a comb on either side of your hair
to set the waves in the right shape. When your
hair is dry, remove the combs (if desired), and
the lift in your hair will remain.

158: For day into evening, carry a small, dressy envelope purse in your briefcase and check the briefcase at the restaurant.

159: If you are too thin, details like gathers, tucking, and ruffles are great.

160: When traveling, pack basics for layering and bring interesting jewelry to spice up your wardrobe so you won't get bored with your look.

161: To camouflage a heavy ankle, wear the lowest-cut shoe.

ᴡᴡᴡᴡᴡᴡᴡᴡᴡᴡᴡᴡᴡᴡᴡᴡᴡᴡᴡᴡᴡᴡᴡᴡᴡᴡᴡᴡᴡᴡᴡᴡᴡᴡᴡᴡᴡ

162: *There's more to looking your best than clothing. Try never to look frantic or it will be the focus and will undermine your efforts at style.*

ᴡᴡᴡᴡᴡᴡᴡᴡᴡᴡᴡᴡᴡᴡᴡᴡᴡᴡᴡᴡᴡᴡᴡᴡᴡᴡᴡᴡᴡᴡᴡᴡᴡᴡᴡᴡᴡ

163: Shoes with worn-down heels are an instant image breaker.

164: The epitome of self-confidence is to send flowers to a man.

165: If one jacket, pants, or skirt shape seems to really work for you, stick to it. Note the manufacturer and always check out their new lines. Designers tend to cut the same sizes and proportions over and over.

166: A belt with a self-buckle instead of a gold or other metal one will go further in your wardrobe because the buckle does not limit the accessorizing. On the other hand, a metallic buckle can tie in with your jewelry for a finished look.

167: Check the weather and dress accordingly:

If it's raining, wear the outfit that goes with the "rain-proof" pumps

If it's a bleak gray day, wear a bright dress

If it's sunny and glorious, wear your short flippy skirt

If it's hot, don't wear your close-fitting, button-up suit

168: Never wear white or even off-white stockings. They make your legs look chalky and heavier.

169: If a coat or jacket pulls around your shoulders and back even a little bit, don't buy it.

~~~~~~

169: *Our advice is to adjust your outfit and look to each situation. For instance, temporarily give up the wilder side of your wardrobe when you go on a corporate interview.*

~~~~~~

171: Makeup Fix: If you apply a dark foundation to an area of your face, that area will recede. It's a great way to soften a jutting chin or diminish the size of your nose.

172: A quick brush of your teeth after lunch leaves you with a fresh mouth for the afternoon. Brush your teeth once more before going out for the evening. Having fresh breath is even more important than how you look!

173: When shopping, go straight for the item you need before you spend all your money on distractions.

174: Switch a dress's self-belt with a belt with a jeweled buckle. Put on earrings that coordinate and you've changed from day to evening.

175: If a new purchase can only make and improve one outfit in your existing wardrobe, it has to be dynamite to be worth buying.

176: White shoes say you're from "out of town," even during the summer.

177: A bright accessory can punch up an outfit. Think in terms of two touches to make an effective statement: shiny gold in your earrings and on your belt buckle or red in the print of your blouse and in your lipstick.

∿∿∿∿∿∿∿∿∿∿∿∿∿∿∿∿∿∿∿∿∿∿∿∿∿∿∿∿∿∿∿∿∿∿∿

178: *Be your own best friend. Use all the discipline you've got to stop bad habits: funny facial expressions, biting your nails, pulling on your hair. It undermines everything.*

∿∿∿∿∿∿∿∿∿∿∿∿∿∿∿∿∿∿∿∿∿∿∿∿∿∿∿∿∿∿∿∿∿∿∿

179: Choose a handbag in proportion to your body. A shoulder bag should rest slightly below your hipbone.

180: If you want your bust to be the focus, wear:

- **a scoop neckline**
- **knits or soft fabrics**
- **a close fit**
- **logistically placed prints or appliqués**
- **soft colors over distracting brights or disguising blacks**
- **a slightly transparent top**
- **a peek-a-boo lace camisole**

181: Wake up fifteen minutes early. It'll calm down your whole morning routine.

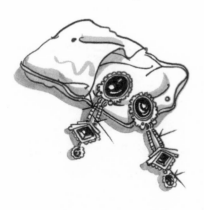

182: Instant day into evening can be as simple as dressy earrings that you keep in your purse at all times. They dress up any outfit.

183: Cool summer chic can be a white shirt:

belted as a tunic

full and smocklike

classic and crisp under a jacket

dressed up with the touch of gold or silver accessories

184: Stop using conditioner if you need more body in your hair to keep that hairstyle.

185: Give your outfit a lift by shortening the hemline.

186: Don't think you've got to have the bust-line you were born with. Go to a good fitter and you'll be amazed by the look the new bras can give you.

187: Modify the trends to what is best for you. If your long hair is out and short is in, cut yours—but maybe only to shoulder length. Don't give up a good feature for a fad.

188: Self-confidence is taking advice well.

189: For a good wardrobe, you only have to buy a few important basics. The most important garment is a super jacket, so buy the best you can afford. Brown, navy, black, beige, and cream will go the furthest.

190: Buy outfits that are appropriate for more than one kind of function. The exception is a black-tie outfit.

191: Definitely buy on impulse if you fall in love with an item. You won't tire of it quickly and you'll look forward to wearing it.

192: If you are short-waisted, a thin belt buckled loosely and pushed down onto your hips will make your waist look longer.

193: How about a new, glamorous shade of hair color? It might allow you to wear totally new clothing colors.

194: If you really want your perfume to last, spray some on a piece of cotton and tuck it into your bra.

195: A little suntan blush on cheeks, chin, nose, and forehead gives an instant healthy look.

196: We don't believe the adage that if you keep something long enough it will come back into style. Some detail will date it—a pleat in the wrong place, a too-wide waistband, or its color.

197: When you want a quality look, gold jewelry always looks richer than silver. If you find it too bright, the antique or brushed-finish look is fine.

198: Changing to better-quality buttons gives an outfit a more expensive look.

199: If you aren't happy with the texture of your hair, switch shampoos. Sometimes a slight difference in ingredients will change the way your hair looks.

200: Each new season, buy one new outfit that makes you feel current and, ideally, can mix with your existing wardrobe. You'll never feel dowdy.

201: A cameo on a velvet ribbon makes a unique choker.

202: The job of a foundation is to create a smooth, flawless, clear palette upon which you can design and emphasize your best features.

203: For Self-Confidence: Take a good look in a full-length mirror before leaving the house in the morning—or before going into a meeting—to make sure your appearance is perfect.

204: Everything in your closet should be visible and uncovered so you can pull things out easily. For instance, all your sweaters should be folded on a shelf near your hanging shirts and pants so that you can see if the colors and textures work together.

205: For day into evening, there is nothing more luxurious than changing into lacy underwear. If you feel beautiful, it will show.

206: Set aside one day to clean out your closet for the next season. Change to the next season's clothes two weeks before everyone else and hear the compliments. You'll feel ahead of the game.

207: Change your bottled makeup once a year because its color can change. Each product has a shelf life and is no longer at its best when that shelf life has expired.

~~~~~~

208: Don't wait until it's too late before you recharge yourself. Keep your image up constantly and your self-confidence will stay up as well.

~~~~~~

209: If a blouse with a front-button closing pulls at all, don't buy it. If you can't button a jacket easily, don't buy it.

210: When people look at you, where do you want them to focus? If your best asset is your face, wear:

a good makeup job

a flattering color near your face

a strong collar that frames your face

outstanding earrings

a choker necklace

a great haircut

a flattering shade of hair color

211: Lip shapes can be corrected:

First, apply foundation and a touch of powder over them

With a sharp lip liner that is close to the color of your lipstick, draw the correcting shape

To make your lips look larger, draw the line just slightly outside the natural line

To make them look smaller, draw just inside

Fill in with lipstick

212: A great dye job is when your hair looks like it's a blend of two to three colors.

213: A closet full of neutrals like beige, gray, and black will mix with anything. It makes shopping for additions less of a guessing game.

214: Remember to use and enjoy all of your clothes. It does you no good to save them for special occasions.

> ***215:*** *We know that it's not just cloth-ing that creates personal style. Posture and body language also help you appear self-confident.*

216: Go through your closet to rescue items and think about using them in different ways. A too-tight sweater can become a favorite blouse substitute under your tweed suit. A dress that doesn't make it anymore for going out at night can become daytime office wear when you change the buttons and add a tailored belt.

217: Don't ever buy a dress that you can't get into by yourself or a dress that's even slightly uncomfortable.

218: A final, cold-water rinse will make your hair shinier.

219: Money-Saving Hint: Try the young men's department for pea jackets, down vests, denim work shirts, tuxedo shirts, rain slickers, or navy sport blazers.

220: Never be down to your last pair of stockings.

221: Self-confidence is not looking at yourself in the mirror when you're in public.

222: Practicality Hint: If you don't see the same people every day, all you need in your closet are two great outfits.

223: Be current. It's spring! Wear your old blazer with a new, short sarong skirt.

224: Match your belt and shoe color. It's an interesting look to mix the different textures of leather and suede, as long as the color matches.

225: When shopping for a specific item, be prepared. Bring along that strapless bra, the right shoe, or the skirt for which you're trying to find a jacket.

226: If you're tall and thin, flared skirts add grace to your height and straight skirts exaggerate it.

227: Savvy Signal: You can update your entire wardrobe with a pair of shoes if they have the latest shape of heel or are in the hottest new color.

228: *We always tell our clients that planning a wardrobe means looking at your life and answering a few basic questions: Do you work? Do you entertain at home? Are restaurants the focus of your social life? Do you belong to a club? Are there business or charity meetings? Do you frequently travel? Is there a man whose opinion counts?*

229: Make your best asset your personal signature, whether it's emphasizing a small waist, good legs, or lovely hair.

230: A quick way to feel feminine right after work is to put on some pearls.

231: Wear a pair of opaque tights under a too-sheer skirt.

233: If you have full hips that you'd rather hide, always add a loose, open top layer, such as a jacket.

234: Don't use nonwaterproof mascara on lower lashes. It smudges into makeup and under-eye cream.

235: If you are tall, tiny prints, delicate jewelry, and sheer fabric will exaggerate your height.

236: When you go to buy a coat, take a jacket with you to try on under the coat and make sure you have enough room.

237: Remove thread belt loops on dresses and replace self-belts—both may reveal how little you paid for an outfit.

238: A Surprise Suggestion: Check out the teenagers. They invent style like no one else. See how they wear a belt, twist a scarf, and combine fabrics and colors. We can learn from them.

239: To keep down unruly hair growth along your hairline or part, spray a cotton ball with hair spray and swab the hairs down—they'll stay!

240: For evening, rhinestone earrings can make your eyes sparkle.

241: For day into evening, wear your suit without a blouse.

242: A good, black faux croc or lizard-textured belt—with a rich-looking gold or silver buckle—is a must have.

243: Another Savvy Signal: Copy a store's window display and the unique way they layer separates. Try putting an old turtleneck under a plaid work shirt and then layer with a sweater tied over your shoulders.

244: Streak some fresh lemon through your hair and sit in the sun for instant highlights.

245: Remove your makeup as carefully as you put it on, with soft strokes always going upward.

246: If you buy a belt with an unusual belt-buckle finish, such as gold and silver together, think about the earrings you intend to wear to finish the outfit, or don't buy that belt.

247: Have one outfit in your favorite bright color—be it red or magenta—always ready to pull out on a bad day.

〰〰〰〰〰〰〰〰〰〰〰〰〰〰〰〰〰〰〰〰〰〰〰〰

248. *Self-confidence is always being willing to help a friend look better.*

〰〰〰〰〰〰〰〰〰〰〰〰〰〰〰〰〰〰〰〰〰〰〰〰

249: Always keep foundation in your skin-tone range or it will appear masklike. The rest of your makeup will also look unnatural, like it's sitting on top of a mask.

250: An evening coat should be seven-eighths length so you can wear it over short dresses, long dresses, and pants.

251: Try a new look in makeup or a different palette of colors, such as all brown-based tones or very pale shades. You'll feel instantly current.

252: Wear a gold or bronze evening belt if your shoes are gold or bronze. Wear silver only with silver. Gold and silver metallics don't mix together well.

253: Give a savvy signal and show you're current with a great new signature haircut.

254: Always make your nails an even length by filing them down to match the shortest one. Short and even beats all different degrees of long.

255: The trick to sticking to exercise is to make it convenient and part of your daily routine.

256: At the beginning of each season, check to see if your wardrobe has an interesting balance of prints and new colors.

257: Fifteen minutes a day of moderate exercise is better than one hour a week of strenuous exercise.

258: When you want to feel more powerful, wear a thicker chain; it makes a stronger statement. Little delicate keepsakes belong inside your clothing.

259: If you are heavy and overblouses are your most flattering line, you can often slit open the two side seams four inches for an easier fit over the hips.

260: For narrower-looking hips, have a tailor remove the inside pocket lining in pants and skirts.

~~~~~~

261: One of our quick formulas for personal style:

> **experiment**
>
> **copy**
>
> **edit**

~~~~~~

262: An experienced traveler never packs any outfit that she hasn't rehearsed. That way she is sure the skirt hem won't be longer than her coat, the shoes that go with it are comfortable, she has the right accessories, and the look works!

263: The ballet slipper is permanently in fashion. With everything from shorts to formal wear, it creates a proportion and look all its own.

264: If you wear glasses, subtract conflicting accessories. The glasses are an accessory themselves.

265: The look of a coatdress is instant chic.

266: The perfect pants length just covers the instep of your foot and hits the top of your shoe with a little break in the pants.

267: An accessory is flattering when:

the earrings conform to facial contours

the necklace lies comfortably around the neck

the belt outlines the waist (doesn't cinch it) or loosely falls on hip curves

the shoes fit the shape of your feet and flatter your legs

the handbag lies against your side and is the right proportion for your body

268: Don't forget about pin curls. They can lift your hair after work when you can't get a hold of your dryer or electric rollers. Spray, pin, and brush out a few minutes later.

269: We've seen that every well-dressed woman eventually goes "classic."

270: If you are heavy, don't wear:

small floral prints

ruffles

small bows

sweet pastels

You'll look larger in contrast.

271: To look instantly pulled together, add a black jacket and a black belt to your wardrobe.

272: An unstructured pant in a jersey or silk is better for casual or dressy wear than for work. Softness lacks authority.

273: When you find a bra that works for you, buy half a dozen. They have a way of disappearing when you look for them in the store again.

274: *Everyone can be sexy and each woman should do it according to her own type. A classic may shorten her skirt to show more leg; a feminine might show lace at her cleavage; an exotic might show bare shoulders. Remember, to feel sexy you've got to be comfortable.*

275: Your shoes determine the mood of your socks or stockings. For instance, wear a walking shoe with country textured stockings.

276: One of the most important reasons to get your body in shape is not for the pounds but for graceful movement and better carriage.

277: Female executives aren't often seen in bright colors; however, the neutrals they choose are not dull, not subtle, not mousy, and certainly not boring, but quietly authoritative. These women mix textures and create style with accessories.

278: If any bra, belt, skirt, or sleeve is tight or uncomfortable, you won't be able to concentrate on your work. Remember that when you are buying clothes.

279: For a change, slip a scarf from the men's department under the lapels of your jacket.

280: Makeup on the beach is inappropriate. Be as natural as you can with waterproof mascara and lip gloss.

281: If you are small busted, go for a looser, relaxed top rather than a stretch bodysuit.

282: An Easy Formula: If the color of your jacket or over layer matches the color of your skirt or pants, your inside blouse or sweater can then be a contrasting color, and it's hard to make a mistake.

283: No black panties under white clothes or vice versa, even if you think you can't see through the fabrics. Others might be able to.

284: Don't ever allow the stirrup of your stirrup pants to be exposed. Hide them with pushed-down socks or low boots.

285: Nails that are not well groomed detract from your style. Keep them perfect with emery boards, hand cream, polish remover, cuticle scissors, base coat and polish, preferably in a light, natural color.

286: An evening shawl can add a flash of dramatic color or print and works with any hemline. And you can keep it with you for the evening and save yourself the trouble of checking your coat.

287: A textured top, such as a woven sweater, can add as much interest as a print when worn under an untextured jacket, such as a flannel.

~~~~~~

288: *Chewing gum is the great image breaker.*

~~~~~~

289: To have a smooth line, tuck your tops into your pantyhose—you can still pull out your top evenly all around for that bloused, relaxed look—and it will stay.

290: A cuffless pants always makes the leg look longer.

291: Coordinated lingerie is the perfect backdrop for coordinated clothing.

292: Once a week give your face a treatment:

> **Exfoliate with a cleanser using gentle cleansing grains**
>
> **Use a mask on your skin for fifteen minutes**
>
> **Use moisturizer and get a good night's sleep**

293: A hair-saving idea for a last-minute special occasion is to slick back your hair with gel (long or short) and do your best makeup job. Finally, add a dynamite pair of earrings to finish off your sophisticated, exotic look.

294: Always stand up straight. Poor posture changes the shape and design of your clothing.

295: A glamorous way to wear a touch of metallic is to make it matte—such as a steel-gray bodysuit or burnished bronze pumps.

296: Makeup Tip: Curve the corners of your mouth upward with your lip liner and lipstick. You'll always have a pleasant expression.

297: For a change, wear a long jacket with a short skirt or wear a short bolero jacket with an ankle-length skirt.

298. *What we think "style" means:*

Your clothes look like they belong to you

Your accessories polish your look

Your makeup is quietly correct

**Your beauty allows your personal charm
to show through**

∿∿∿

299: Eye-shadow technique for every shape eye: Stroke on a light base all over the lid. Place a medium-tone shadow in the outer corner and drag it about one-third toward the center. Line the crease with the medium tone, blend gently, and you're done.

300: Beauty routines that are a must:

Moisturize your face

Rub creamy lotion on your hands and feet

Shampoo frequently

Get a manicure, a pedicure, and a waxing as regularly as you can

301: A skin-toned body stocking works magic under any sheer or cut-out fabric.

~~~~~~

302: *Sometimes you're saying something about yourself and don't even know it. For instance, too many grays and blacks give a sophisticated but drab message.*

~~~~~~

303: Often a ribbon can function very well on a party dress if you don't have the right evening belt.

304: Good Storage Care: Stuff the following with tissue paper:

evening gown sleeves and fragile blouse sleeves

pouch purses

strappy shoes

hats

305: To feel feminine, try putting some waves in your hair.

306: If you've got a great rear:

Wear well-fitted pants and tucked-in tops

Wear bias-cut skirts in a soft, supple fabric

Wear slightly higher heels to remind yourself to walk more gracefully

307: For an instant lift, highlight your hair. You can bet it will bring light to your face.

308: All necklaces can hang from hooks on a wall like artwork—they are then easy to see and easy to pull.

309: If your limbs are long and your sleeves are too short, go for the pushed-up or rolled-up sleeve look.

310: Keep all items that need alterations together and pull them out to fix when you are watching your favorite movie on TV.

〰〰〰〰〰〰〰〰〰〰〰〰〰〰〰〰〰〰〰〰〰〰〰〰〰〰

311: Having a beautiful smile no longer has to cost a fortune. Check with your dentist for all the affordable new ways to improve your teeth.

〰〰〰〰〰〰〰〰〰〰〰〰〰〰〰〰〰〰〰〰〰〰〰〰〰〰

312: Accessories should never be the focus. They should lead the eye to your face.

313: Highlighting allows you to go a little longer before the gray hair starts showing.

314: Don't be afraid to switch products. Even though you like a particular makeup, technology is always developing new products and one may be more effective for you. Experiment. You can always go back.

315: Replace your suit blouse with a black or cream satiny camisole. It is the most important item to own that says day into evening.

316: A quick day into evening makeup fix: Don't start over from scratch with your makeup, simply:

apply a deeper blush

add some shadow to the outside corners of your eyes

add a coat of mascara

reline lips and reapply lipstick

~~~~~~

317: *We tell our clients: Wearing curlers anywhere outside of the home (car included) is inappropriate.*

~~~~~~

318: Sometimes all you need is a trim to lighten the weight of your hair. It can look bouncier and healthier immediately.

319: To relax before a big evening, take a bubble bath with bath oil, soft music, and scented candles. Try to soak for at least ten minutes.

320: To avoid being identified as wearing one designer's look, buy the main pieces that you like, then shop creatively to add some small additional items of memorable texture or color from another source.

321: To get the most out of cleaning out your closet:

Put on your makeup and actually try on outfits

Write down the good combinations

Remove any piece or outfit that doesn't make it; write yourself a note, if necessary, to replace it

Compare one garment to another to help clarify the quality level you should maintain

Finally, organize your closet. Hang all suits together, dresses together, skirts together, pants together, and blouses together so you can coordinate easily

322: Never wear shorts, sneakers, or tights to work no matter how casual your company is.

323: For a quick touch of style, add an exaggerated accessory like a huge hair bow, an outstanding belt buckle, or a bold necklace or pin.

~~~~~~

324: *We see women's roles in society constantly changing, so our recommendation is that everyone take an image assessment every three years. You'll probably need to make some adjustments to reflect the changing you.*

~~~~~~

325: If you don't think your legs are great and you want to wear short skirts, wear dark opaque hose in winter and taupe opaque hose in summer.

326: A facial is something that you deserve! It will work for you as it cleans, softens, and revitalizes your skin.

327: Have a second set of your cosmetics ready for travel. It doesn't mean you have to buy all new items. When a product is three-fourths used up, put it right into your travel cosmetic case and you'll have that second set ready.

328: Heels that tap when you walk are instant image breakers.

329: Think of your voice as a musical instrument and be aware of keeping its pitch perfect.

330: For a quick lift, apply blush on your cheekbones. It lifts the focus and takes attention away from drooping lines.

331: A baseball cap makes a fun sun hat and creates a great youthful look.

332: For a unique look that is all your own, try wearing fabrics out of season, like organza in winter or pale suede in summer.

333: If you wear a strong eyeglass prescription, get the new ultrathin lenses if you can.

334: Have a great home uniform, something to slip into that is attractive as well as comfortable.

∿∿∿∿∿∿∿∿∿∿∿∿∿∿∿∿∿∿∿∿∿∿∿∿∿∿∿∿∿∿∿∿∿∿

335: *At work, avoid:*

> **low necklines**
>
> **clinging clothes**
>
> **see-through garments**
>
> **glitter**
>
> **tight fits**

∿∿∿∿∿∿∿∿∿∿∿∿∿∿∿∿∿∿∿∿∿∿∿∿∿∿∿∿∿∿∿∿∿∿

336: Neutrals together—such as beige with cream or taupe with black—are always chic.

337: Roll a little silk or wool undershirt in your tote if you're going to an air-conditioned place later and you think you might get cold. Always pack it in your suitcase when traveling anywhere.

338: One elegant silk scarf combining your neutrals is a lot better than a drawer full of scarves in colors that aren't in your closet.

339: If you are too thin, wear fabrics with some body. Stay away from clinging fabrics like jersey.

340: Don't shop for the outfit on the same day you have to wear it to an important evening event.

341: In hot weather, change from opaque black to sheer skin-tone hose—certainly make the switch by April.

342: If you "wear well" in your voice, clothing, and attitude, people will want you around.

343: Don't use woven straw or canvas totes for work. They're too casual.

344: If you are petite and slim, you can wear very current avant-garde clothes. They may look better on you than on a bigger body!

345: If you have a small bust, bring the focus upward to strong square shoulders. Try shoulder pads.

346: *You'll receive better treatment from everyone—from a lawyer to a maître d'— if you're well dressed.*

347: Self-confidence is having great "shoulders back" posture.

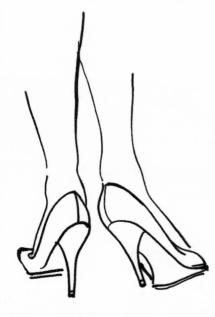

348: Keep a pair of black pumps with the highest heel you are comfortable wearing at the office for unexpected evening dates. Nothing says "dress up" more than a graceful high heel.

349: Your best colors are usually the ones that match your personality:

For shy personalities, soft colors are best

For friendly, outgoing personalities, medium-bright colors are best

For dramatic personalities, jewel tones or black are best

For quiet personalities, subdued tones are best

For practical, classic personalities, neutrals are best

350: A few pieces of real jewelry can make all your other jewelry look better.

351: Makeup Tip: A light foundation color is always a better choice than a dark one, which may muddy your skin.

352: Ordinary suits fail in two ways: They are no fun and they don't carry enough clout. Buy a better suit.

353: *Our society demands instant impressions, so focus on how you want to come across in that first moment you enter a room. Don't only dress for it, act the part!*

354: When you take a pen out of your purse, it becomes an accessory. It should be carefully chosen.

355: In summer, a metallic off-color shoe is a nice change from heavy black or brown.

356: Start shopping in August for winter clothes and in March for spring clothes. But remember to change your closets first, so you won't be duplicating any item you already own.

357: Instant Current: Add a skinny belt over a fitted suit jacket.

358: Image Maker: Choose your personal stationery as if it were part of your wardrobe. It gives any message you want it to.

359: A straight, classic coat is best for most proportions. If it's black it will complement most outfits from casual daywear to black tie.

360: For great makeup organization, fill a basket with your makeup tools. Empty it out when you're ready to do your face. As you put each item back after you use it, you'll know you didn't skip a step.

361: For an instant style change: Wear your suit with only its vest underneath, and no blouse.

362: *Copy something from a person you admire—her lipstick color, her always-perfect hose color, the way she takes the time to pull herself together. The right role model is better than a subscription to any fashion magazine.*

363: Buy only a foundation with sunblock.

364: If you want your eyes to stand out, line the outer two-thirds of your eye, top and bottom, and then smudge the lines to soften the effect. Brown, charcoal, or navy are good colors to use.

365: Keep the mood of the outfit when you accessorize. If you are stuck, go with a plain stud earring.

366: For short waists, always use the trick of blousing your tops rather than tucking them in tightly. Blousing can make the top of your body look an inch and a half longer.

367: Packing is a lot simpler if you start at the bottom. Coordinate your outfits around the least number of pairs of comfortable shoes you plan to take.

368: As your budget grows, spend money on alterations. To get the full value from an expensive outfit it should fit perfectly. Although it's hard to add to an already steep price, the investment will pay off.

369: Day to evening: Exchange your suit blouse for a gold choker on bare skin, and gold earrings.

~~~~~~

370: We believe in personal routines. A solid daily grooming ritual will eventually become essential to a woman in maintaining good mental health.

~~~~~~

371: Balanced shine in accessories means coordinating your earrings, belt buckle, watch, ring, and bracelet. One should lead the eye to the other and none should stand out significantly.

372: Don't wear perfume to the gym. It's a place where a natural body scent is best.

373: If you are too tall or too long-waisted, break up the length by wearing an interesting belt.

374: Just changing to a slightly higher heel will make you walk with a lighter step than a flat. It will also serve as a reminder to stand taller.

375: It's amazing how a small squirt of hair spray keeps your hairstyle all day. During the day just use a little water and run your fingers through your hair to reactivate it.

376: Schedule all important meetings for the morning, when you look your freshest.

377: When you pack, bring outfits you can layer for colder weather and for a change of look.

378: The best way to use blush as a contour is to suck in your cheeks and apply a slightly darker shade in the natural hollow.

379: Study the merchandise in the best stores even if your budget can't afford them. You will learn to look for similar merchandise characteristics in a store you can afford.

380: To smooth your feet, rub on a heavy cream and wear cotton socks overnight.

381: For a change, silver jewelry looks more creative after work and on weekends.

382: If your arms are too thin, avoid sleeveless tops or tight, fitted sleeves and go for elbow-length or fuller, soft sleeves.

383: Great haircuts can eliminate bad hair days.

384: Color Trick: Wearing tone on tone—such as gray with gray—gives a long, slim look. It makes you look taller than a contrasting top and bottom like gray and black.

385: Spray perfume on your skin, not on your clothes.

386: Self-confidence is taking criticism well.

387: When you shop, don't think about losing ten pounds before you buy an outfit. If it looks good, buy it. It will only look better once you've lost the weight.

388: Reorganize your closet on a different day than when you clean your house. You'll need all your energy for the project.

389: A Savvy Signal: Try this for a different color combination—brown with red or gray with chartreuse.

390: Each season, if you can't afford a whole outfit, buy one new item. Pick something that makes you feel current, such as a metallic color bodysuit or a flippy chiffon skirt.

~~~~~~

391: *When putting together a client's wardrobe, we make sure she buys a few pieces that reach beyond her present level of style, for example, a seven-eighths coat instead of a jacket or a lacy camisole instead of a blouse.*

~~~~~~

392: Whenever you wear dark, sheer hose, bring an extra pair in case you get a run—nothing looks worse.

393: When money is tight, make your wardrobe go the furthest by owning a light neutral set (beige blouse and pant) and a dark neutral set (black sweater and skirt). All the pieces will mix and match—with each other and with everything else you have.

394: Add a third layer of a vest, jacket, sweater, or shawl to hide figure flaws of a wide waist, a short waist, or large hips. You'll be adding some dash at the same time.

395: Good tailoring is more visible and therefore more important in a solid than in a pattern.

396: The greatest luxury is to have tiny snaps put on all shoulder pads so that they are always in place and can be easily removed when you send the item to the cleaner.

397: Go and buy that expensive designer outfit instead of wasting money on all those compromises that don't satisfy you.

398: Use your choice of fragrance to change your own mood, as well as that of others around you.

~~~~~~

399: *We Believe in Touch-Ups: A quick application of lipstick and face powder is okay in public. (The embarrassing thing that happens next is that every woman at the table will follow the lead and all will be powdering and fixing at the same time!) Anything more, like brushing your hair, should take place in the washroom.*

~~~~~~

400: A little natural shine on your face is more youthful than a powdered-down look.

401: Petites should steer clear of the little-girl look or any look that's too stiff and fitted.

402: Bring out the ends of brows to make your eyes look longer.

403: When you're wearing all one color, you might want to incorporate a different texture for interest.

404: If you have to pull last season's suit out for an emergency and the skirt's too long, go ahead, roll the waist over this one time. But afterward, go straight to the tailor for a new hem.

‍‍‍‍‍‍‍‍‍‍‍‍‍‍‍‍

***405:** We try to help our clients accept their body types. No diet can change the length of a leg, the placement of a waist, the thickness of a neck. Learn to work with what you have.*

406: When traveling, carry with you anything that is essential and don't depend on your luggage getting there.

407: If you think you are heavy, pay even more attention to your hair and makeup, because this is where you want to bring the focus.

408: Carry a silk scarf in your bag. This serves as a quick fix to dress up or add warmth to an outfit, as a hair tie, or as a cover for a bare neckline when it's suddenly not appropriate.

~~~~~~

409: *Having style is knowing what to wear in every situation—such as pulling out that classic velvet jacket for the last-minute client dinner.*

~~~~~~

410: For a quick lift to an old suit, there is nothing like a pin, perhaps one you've lovingly collected.

411: With shorter, cooler showers, you'll remove less oil from your body.

412: If you are large, outgoing, and look great in colors, go ahead and get away from only wearing darks.

413: Clothes affect our mannerisms and the way we move. Tighter-fitting clothes make you move with more awareness. Every once in a while it's not a bad reminder.

414: Straps on a camisole or dress that are too loose will cause you to tense your shoulders to keep them in place, which can be exhausting—shorten the straps.

415: Makeup Note: Always apply eye make-up with upward strokes to avoid pulling the skin downward.

416: If you are short, avoid long hem lengths and heavy shoes. Both will bring the focus downward and make you seem shorter.

417: Don't try to save money on dry cleaners. The worst thing you can do to an expensive outfit is use a home remedy. It is not worth what it may cost you in the end.

418: Easy Evening Uniform: Black crepe evening pants with a variety of tops and glamorous accessories.

~~~~~~

419: A sophisticated fashion rule we try to show our clients is that some garments have intrinsic integrity. If a safari jumpsuit isn't olive-drab, it's not a safari jumpsuit. If you like it better in hot pink, stop yourself from buying it.

~~~~~~

420: An accessory can tie a whole outfit together. A black blouse worn with a red-and-black-print skirt can be chic when finished with a red belt.

421: Merge some femininity with practicality. Change to pearl buttons on your cardigan sweater.

422: Super Tip: Always wear your clothing a little bigger if you want to look smaller. They will simply hang better.

423: Being feminine is having a soft voice that never becomes a whisper.

424: If you think your lips are large, wear a less bright shade in a matte lipstick.

425: Remember to indulge your hands with rich hand lotion and they'll stay young.

~~~~~~

426: *Making the latest fashion statement when you're with people whose lifestyle is simpler is inappropriate.*

~~~~~~

427: If you own only two jackets: One should be a dark solid to go over any tweed or patterned bottom. The second should be a textured tweed or check to go with the other half of your wardrobe, the solid skirts and pants.

428: You can always have the shoemaker lower your high heels by one lift without ruining the balance of the shoe.

429: A bright red lipstick can make your teeth look yellow, but a blue-red makes them look whiter.

430: Change shoes to preserve energy. Change into a pair of flats when you have to do a lot of walking. Changing heel heights can be almost as effective as a nap!

~~~~~~

431: Self-confidence is keeping a friend's secret to yourself. You'll end up being better friends.

~~~~~~

432: The look of a colorful scarf in a neckline can be great, but it can also become too much of a formula. Vary your necklaces, and sometimes just leave your neck bare.

433: If your waist is wide or if you have big hips, you can still wear a belt, but add a top layer of a loose, open jacket. Only the finishing touch of the buckle will show.

434: A long, narrow, white silk scarf with fringe will instantly dress up a suit or a coat. It also works for black-tie outfits.

435: Once in a while, don't carry an evening bag to dinner or a party. It's a young look that says: "I don't have to check my hair or makeup."

436: If you're wearing a lot of necklace, choose simple earrings to finish your look.

437: It is usually a more balanced look when the darker color is worn on the bottom.

438: *Enjoy the whole experience. Dress to please yourself as well as your audience. You must always be comfortable. Self-confidence is the glow that has got to be there.*

439: If you smile when you talk on the phone, your self-confidence will come through.

440: Remembering someone's name is like giving them a gift.

441: Practice your outfit if the occasion is important. Put it on exactly the way you are going to wear it. Move around and sit down in it. It may take time now, but it will be worth it later.

442: A full-length mirror can be your best friend. You'll learn to recognize the correct proportions of skirt, pants, and jacket and which proportions best suit your body.

443: Best Buy: Fabrics that can be worn ten months of the year—like crepe or lightweight gabardine in nonseasonal colors like taupe and black—are the most versatile and classic.

444: If you can't find the right necklace and earrings for that evening dress, you can always wear a fresh flower on your shoulder or in your hair.

⁓⁓

445: *Self-confidence is always being ready to accept an engagement.*

⁓⁓

446: A sophisticated balance is a very tailored jacket in a soft wool crepe and in a lovely pale color.

447: Sometimes what seems inappropriate is intriguing, like a summer white crepe pantsuit at a winter cocktail party.

448: When you return from a trip, immediately make a list of things you forgot to take. Add them to the original list of essential things you need to pack every time you take a trip. Tape the list to the inside of your suitcase.

449: If your hair seems to be limp from over-conditioning, strip it with a pure baby shampoo to get rid of the buildup. Use the baby shampoo a few times before going back to your usual routine.

450: If you tend to freeze in front of your closet, choose your clothes the night before.

451: Luggage-tan-colored belt, bag, and shoes can be a great balance trick for redheads.

ⵡⵡⵡⵡⵡⵡⵡⵡⵡⵡⵡⵡⵡⵡⵡⵡⵡⵡⵡⵡⵡⵡⵡⵡⵡⵡⵡⵡⵡⵡⵡ

450: *Use your clothing as a personal tool. Always be ready for that unexpected meeting. If you keep up a personal standard in the way you look everyday, you will never be caught unprepared.*

ⵡⵡⵡⵡⵡⵡⵡⵡⵡⵡⵡⵡⵡⵡⵡⵡⵡⵡⵡⵡⵡⵡⵡⵡⵡⵡⵡⵡⵡⵡⵡ

453: An occasional professional pedicure will pay for itself as it saves the life of your hose and smoothes your feet for shoe comfort.

454: Stay away from iridescent eye shadows if you want to de-emphasize wrinkles and sagging lids.

455: A minimal jewelry wardrobe includes a good gold necklace and earring set and a more casual silver necklace and earring set. (When we say "set," the pieces don't have to be an exact match but must complement each other.)

456: Anchor all scarves the way you want them to look on your shoulders with small safety pins and you won't have to think about and fuss with them.

457: Straight skirts are more flattering when tapered in at the bottom on both sides.

458: Another Image Rule: Even on "dress-down Friday" wear the third layer of a jacket or a vest if you want to keep your authority.

459: If you are impatient, use a fast-drying top coat on your nails and then dip your hands into ice water.

460: From May to September, change from dark brown leather accessories to luggage brown, light tan, or taupe.

461: The best long-sleeve length is just below the wrist bone.

∿∿∿

462. *Self-confidence is giving away a personal beauty secret.*

∿∿∿

463: In summer, a white vee- or jewel-neck short-sleeved cotton T-shirt is a must. It works under a suit for an instant update, and goes out on its own in the evening with some chunky jewelry and any bottom.

464: Keep a very small folding umbrella in your bag. It pays off.

465: An instant lift can be achieved with a dash of color in a belt, especially if you are known for neutrals.

466: Another Image Rule: Never buy it unless the item says something you want to say about yourself.

467: If you can, choose just one fragrance out of the multitudes. It's great to always be recognized for your unique scent.

468: Never try any new makeup when you have to look terrific. Practice on a regular day with no pressure.

469: At certain stressful events, you are going to need to be especially comfortable. Plan your outfit and shoes with comfort in mind. You never want to undermine yourself by being or appearing uncomfortable.

470: The best crisis moisturizer for every part of your body is Vaseline. Apply it, go to sleep, and it will start its magic.

471: More than two rings on one hand shouts distraction.

~~~~~~

472: *Self-confidence is giving a friend something of yours that she admires.*

~~~~~~

473: For a more authoritative look, try small, sophisticated geometric prints rather than florals.

474: The easiest trick to avoiding wrinkles when packing is to fold the garment right in the plastic bag it came in from the cleaners or to use layers of tissue paper.

475: High heels with shorts, Bermudas, or casual long pants are always inappropriate.

476: Anything too short is inappropriate.

477: Jewelry with a bathing suit is inappropriate.

478: Each night, lay out the next day's outfit with matching shoes, hosiery, and accessories.

479: If you haven't worn something for two seasons, give it away for a tax deduction. You'll never feel great in it and that's the feeling you're going for with each outfit.

480: A Sophisticated Balance: If the dress has a lower neckline than you are used to, choosing it in a dark color will make you feel less vulnerable.

481: It is a nice idea to change your scent when you are ending one chapter in your life and beginning another.

482: For instant authority, always choose a great suit.

483: Tape-record your voice. Just say your name, what you do, and where you live. Then listen to what will sound like a complete stranger and correct the flaws.

484: It may not have been your best look before, but lately have you tried:

bangs?

red nails?

bigger jewelry?

a little longer hem length?

paler makeup?

485: Try not to buy more clothes than you have time to wear. It's no fun to have clothes with tags go through a season in your closet unworn.

∿∿

486: *Clients tell us that they have so much extra time for themselves after we help them pare down and simplify their beauty and dressing routines.*

∿∿

487: Your highest heel must allow you to walk with a confident, easy gait and never be so high as to throw off your body alignment.

488: It may be your favorite color, but sometimes a whole expanse of it is too much, for instance, an orange suit.

489: If you have a beauty mark in a good place—above your lip or on your cheekbone— enhance it gently with a light brown pencil and then blot it.

490: For a change, dress up a traditional beige gabardine raincoat with a beautiful paisley- print scarf. The raincoat is a backdrop and should be accessorized with individual flair.

491: Self-confidence is talking less and listening more.

492: To look more interesting, change your textures when layering, for example, a rib with a flat knit or a jacquard pattern with a plain wool.

493: For the look of a longer leg, wear a pump with no straps anywhere. For the longest leg, wear it in taupe with matching hose.

494: Layer two contrasting shirts. Tuck in the inside shirt and tie the ends of the outside shirt in a loose knot. You've got a casual, layered blouson-jacket look.

495: If the button on a one-button jacket is above your natural waistline, your legs will look longer.

496: If you never want to have to change your purse, buy a bag that's brown with black trim or vice versa. The predominant color should be the shoe color you usually wear.

497: Curl your eyelashes to open up your eyes. But match the contour of the lash curler to your eye. Each brand is different.

498: One of the best sale items to look for is leather gloves, because they never change and you can always use them.

499: Fashion is synonymous with change. Don't collect too many articles in one style unless it's your signature. The style may be gone before you know it.

~~~~~~

500: **Our Promise: If we can help you conquer your image insecurities and get past the wasted time you spend putting yourself down, you'll have much more positive energy.**

~~~~~~

"We know this book may
leave some of your questions
unanswered . . .

Photograph by Chad Weckler

. . . If you have even the slightest
qualm about your choice of clothes or
the least little doubt about the image
you project—call us for help."

Emily Cho

Neila Fisher

New Image
Consulting Service

P.O. Box 260
Alphine, NJ 07620

201-784-3325